The Wounded Soul:

A Legacy of Healing and Voice Restoration

By

Dr. Barbara J. Tyson

DEDICATION

To my late mother, Church Mother Agnes Walter—whose prayers birthed this ministry. To my seven children, eleven grandchildren, and radiant great-granddaughter—with many more blessings to come. To the wounded, silenced, and displaced: your voice matters. Your healing is holy.

AUTHOR BIO

Dr. Barbara J. Tyson is a Doctor of Christian Philosophy, licensed State Evangelist, and founder of Doctors House LLC. She is a ministry systems architect, healing curriculum designer, voice restoration coach, and author of *The Wounded Soul: A Legacy of Healing and Voice Restoration*.

Her work transforms personal testimony and clinical frameworks into structured healing curriculum for churches, transitional homes, and outreach ministries. It also serves as a professional resource for therapists, mental health clinicians, and substance-abuse recovery coaches who guide others through emotional and spiritual restoration. She offers online coaching for individuals and groups, specializing in adults and young adults ages 18–32. Her coaching integrates biblical truth, prophetic insight, and evidence-based modalities such as CBT and DBT.

Dr. Tyson also leads online prophetic prayer sessions, creating safe spaces for spiritual intercession, voice restoration, and breakthrough. A former radio host turned podcast architect, she continues to amplify healing through voice-based ministry and digital outreach.

She honors her spiritual lineage, church covering, and the memory of her late husband, Deacon Lamont Tyson; her father, Henry Walter; and her beloved mother, the late Church Mother Agnes Walter, whose faith laid the foundation for her ministry. She is the proud mother of seven children, grandmother to eleven, and great-grandmother to one radiant great-granddaughter—with many more blessings expected to come.

Her ministry reaches across generations, serving youth, widows, recovering families, and ministry leaders with compassion, strategy, and discernment. Every release is a prophetic offering, designed to restore voice, belonging, and legacy to the wounded and overlooked.

She is the baby of four siblings: her elder sister, Virgina Walter-Anderson, the late Linda Lou Walter, and the late Henry Walter Jr.

ACKNOWLEDGMENTS

To **Archbishop Leonard Naylor** and **Overseer Charlene Naylor** of *Holy Redeemer Cathedral, Springfield, MA 01107*— I have been a faithful member since **October 7, 1991**, and my life has never been the same. You spiritually birthed me, covered me, and entrusted me with the mantle of healing. You trained me, released me, and allowed me to serve as **Clinical Director of the Deborah House for Women and Children**, a ministry under your leadership. For ten years, I volunteered in that sacred assignment— helping battered women, incarcerated mothers, and those in recovery or active addiction find their way back to life.

You gave me room to grow, space to heal, and a platform to serve. Through your unwavering faith and spiritual authority, I witnessed transformation. Families were restored. Hope was reborn. And I was never the same.

To my oldest daughter, **Dr. Malissa Naylor**, at just nine years old you had the courage to bring me before the Pastor and the Lord. After their prayer, I experienced a spiritual awakening at my apartment. I woke out of a slumber, and a voice spoke to me: "It is now time out." That moment changed everything. You stood in the gap so your siblings could have a healed mother—and not have to bury me before my time.

Your bravery opened the door to my salvation. Your obedience to the Holy Spirit visited my apartment and spoke to me time out led me to the church. And God saved me. Because of you, I live. Because of you, I heal. Because of you, I now help others do the same.

I also want to acknowledge all my children's, names Toren, Cassie, Cornelius, Dorcas, Isha, and Lamont Jr whose presence and support have been a blessing in this journey.

This acknowledgment is not just gratitude—it is generational honor. You are part of the legacy I now release into the world.

TABLE OF CONTENTS

Back Matter

Appendix A: Healing Scriptures

A curated list of verses for grief, trauma, anxiety, and restoration.

Appendix B: Coaching Intake Form

For individual and group coaching clients ages 18–32.

Appendix C: Legacy Archive Checklist

Steps to organize your testimony, manuscripts, and ministry materials.

ABOUT THE AUTHOR

Dr. Barbara J. Tyson is a voice restoration coach, curriculum designer, and founder of Doctors House LLC. She offers coaching, prophetic prayer, and healing curriculum for churches, transitional homes, and outreach ministries.

Contact & Ministry Resources

Website: [Insert URL] Email: [Insert Email] Podcast: *Voice Restored* Prayer Line: [Insert Number] Social Media: @DrBarbaraTyson

CHAPTER 1

THE FAMILY SCROLL:

What Tried to Break Us, What God Preserved

My story begins long before I learned the sound of my own voice. It begins with a lineage marked by both endurance and affliction. It begins with a family that carried burdens greater than its years. My mother was the eldest of ten, a girl who became a caretaker before she ever became a woman. She was raised under a hard hand by a mother whose anger spoke louder than affection, whose drinking drowned tenderness, and whose distance bred duty. My mother learned to be strong, but not safe. She learned to serve, but not to rest.

When she married, she believed love would rewrite her beginning. Yet the ghosts of responsibility followed her into every room. Marriage did not erase the weight she carried; it merely gave it new names. Somewhere between survival and surrender, another spirit entered, Aida Sheffield. She was charming, but cunning. A woman who dabbled in darkness, practicing voodoo and summoning division. She buried objects in our yard, chanted curses, and desired my father for herself. What began as suspicion became separation.

Aida's influence infected what should have been sacred. She claimed a child by my father, it was a child whose very body bore witness to deceit. The head was swollen with water, the features unrecognizable, and yet she insisted it was his. That lie became the wedge that split generations. My family fractured under whispers and warfare which was spiritual, emotional, and unseen.

Through those years, I watched my mother bear pain with grace and grit. She loved beyond betrayal. She served beyond strength. I inherited both her tenderness and her tenacity, the ache and the anointing. I did not know then that what she could not carry would become my calling.

Generational wounds have a way of disguising themselves as normalcy. We pass them down like heirlooms, polishing dysfunction until it shines like tradition. But God has always been in the business of preservation. What the enemy orchestrated for destruction, He kept for deliverance.

This family scroll is not just my history—it is my inheritance. Every story of abuse, abandonment, and attack has been rewritten by grace. The curses have been confronted; the cycles have been broken. What tried to destroy my bloodline became the blueprint for my ministry.

If you're reading this and see your own reflection in these pages, know this: you were never forgotten in the chaos that shaped you. God was there—in the silence, in the split, in the struggle—writing redemption between every line.

What tried to break you is about to become the evidence of what God preserved.

And though my family's wounds ran deep, my own story was just beginning. Let's begin.

CHAPTER 2

CHILDHOOD WOUNDS:

The Lost Key & Buried Dreams.

Yet even before those silent ministry years, there was a little girl crying for her key.

I cried out, again and again, for the key to my diary. It was the one place I could pour out my heart. It wasn't where I left it. I searched, pleaded, asked over and over, but no one seemed to hear me. The noise of adults drowned out my voice.

First it was my pencil. I told myself, "It's just a pencil, there are more." But the key was different. The key was sacred. It unlocked my dreams, my thoughts, my truth. And when it disappeared, something inside me disappeared too. That was the moment my dreams were stolen.

I didn't choose abuse but abuse chose me. Circumstances that I never invited shaped me without my permission. I was emotionally, socially, and nutritionally neglected. From that neglect, I learned to neglect myself. It felt normal. It felt like survival.

So, when I grew old enough to reach for alcohol and cocaine, it seemed like I had finally found a way to hurt myself and feel good at the same time. I didn't know it was destruction. I thought it was relief.

Around people, I felt fear. The fear of being seen and judged. I wasn't accepted or expected to be part of anything whole or healthy. My siblings had a foundation I did not. I noticed it. I felt it. I lived it. And so, I withdrew, or I drank too much. I ended the party not because I didn't know how else to be. It seemed like control. Until it wasn't. And then I was alone again.

Even food became a wound. Raised on fast food like grinders, hot dogs, French fries, fried chicken, bacon, soda, this was my diet, and it shaped me in ways I am still healing from. Abuse was handed to me in a paper bag, and I carried its effects long into adulthood.

But my story didn't end there. My dreams weren't stolen forever; they were buried. Buried under ignorance, shame, and fear. And then God's love found me. A love that does not judge, a love that forgives, covers, renews, and restores. His grace was sufficient. His love was perfect.

This chapter is for the ones who feel their childhood still cries out for healing. For the ones who have buried dreams under survival. For the ones who think they've lost too much to ever be whole again.

Your story is not finished. The Spirit still leads, even in wounds, and He knows how to restore what was lost.

CHAPTER 3

THE WOUNDS THAT FOLLOWED ME:

Abuse did not end with childhood but instead it traveled with me. It taught me how to hurt myself even when no one else was hurting me.

I learned to silence my needs because my needs were never met. I learned to numb myself with substances because pain became familiar. What began in neglect became my own pattern of destruction.

Emotional neglect carved deep valleys in my soul. Social rejection convinced me I was always on the outside looking in. Nutritional neglect weakened not just my body but my sense of worth. Each of these wounds became a voice, telling me I wasn't enough.

I thought I had buried those voices, but they followed me into every room. They whispered when I was alone, and they shouted when I tried to belong. My past wasn't just behind me; it was inside me, shaping my choices and my silence.

Dreams were buried, but not dead. Even in the middle of self-destruction, God's love pursued me. His whisper cut through the noise: *"You are mine."*

Grace met me in the rubble. Mercy covered me when shame wanted to expose me. Love rebuilt me when I thought I was beyond repair.

This chapter is for the ones who feel their wounds never stay buried. For the ones who believe they will never escape the cycle. For the ones who hear old voices telling them they are broken beyond repair.

You are not your wounds.

You are God's beloved.

Healing is not only possible but it has already begun.

CHAPTER 4

WHEN THE CHURCH WOUNDS:

Breaking the Silence Before I ever preached, taught, or coached, I sat in pews with a broken heart and a silenced voice. I didn't know how to name the pain, but I felt it every time someone judged me without knowing my story. Every time I was overlooked, dismissed, or labeled. The church is supposed to be a hospital—but sometimes, it becomes the place where the wounded are ignored.

I've seen people exposed publicly in the name of correction, but what it produced was shame, not healing. I've watched leaders speak truth without love, and saints offer scripture without compassion. I've been the girl in the corner, the woman on the back row, the soul who showed up hoping for grace but received silence instead.

But God never stopped speaking. Even when people failed me, His Spirit kept drawing me. He didn't call me to run from the church—He called me to help restore it. Not with arrogance, but with understanding. Not with judgment, but with compassion.

Healing from church wounds requires honesty. It requires us to say, "Yes, I was hurt," without letting that hurt define our future. It requires us to forgive without pretending it didn't happen. And most of all, it requires us to return—not to the same pew, but to the presence of God.

This chapter is for the ones who were wounded in the place they thought was safe. For the ones who almost gave up on God because of people. For the ones who are still sitting quietly, wondering if anyone sees them.

I see you.

God sees you.

And healing is still possible.

Let's walk through it together.

CHAPTER 5

BURIED DREAMS & SPIRITUAL AWAKENING:

My dreams were not stolen forever but they were buried. I thought they were gone, but they were only hidden under years of neglect and pain.

God's love found me in the burial ground. It was not judgment that uncovered me, but grace. Grace sufficient. Love perfect. Mercy unending.

The same God who watched me bury my voice came to restore it. The same God who saw me bury my dreams breathed life back into them. He showed me that what was buried could bloom again.

Being born again was not just a spiritual expression. It was the truth of my life. Change is possible. A new beginning is real. I was broken, but He made me whole. I was a sacrifice, but He turned my sorrow into joy.

I discovered that wounds are not the end of the story but they are the soil where God plants healing. Transformation is not about erasing what happened; it is about redeeming it. And redemption is exactly what God did.

This chapter is for the ones who think too much has been lost. For the ones who believe their dreams are buried too deep. For the ones who have mistaken silence for death.

Your story is not over.

Your dreams are not gone.

And your awakening is already here.

CHAPTER 6

FROM BROKENNESS TO GLORY

I start on the inside — where the wounds hide, where the silence screams, where the soul aches.

Most people try to heal from the outside in, but you can't lead someone where you haven't been.

You can't heal what you haven't faced.

I've experienced real deliverance. I've walked through real healing. And healing is real.

Ask me how I know? Because God did it.

Every good thing that ever happened to me — God did it.

Every breakthrough, every restoration, every moment of peace — God did it.

If He could heal me, He can heal you too. This mantle isn't borrowed; it's birthed.

And I wear it with reverence, with power, and with purpose.

Archbishop Leonard Naylor and Overseer Charlene Naylor of Holy Redeemer Cathedral in Springfield, Massachusetts — they did a work on me.

What the world called a crackhead; they saw as a soul. They looked at me through the eyes of God — not through judgment, but through divine vision.

Glory be to God.

I wasn't a crackhead; I was a victim of my own abuse. There's a difference.

And that difference matters, because when you start judging others, you miss the story — and when you miss the story, you miss the glory God wants to reveal.

Everyone deserves a chance. Everyone deserves their hour to know who Jesus is.

So, soul-winner, do the work. Go ye and preach the gospel — to the rich, to the poor, to the hurting, to the hungry.

Bless you. This is the mantle. This is the mission. This is the movement.

CHAPTER 7

MY CHURCH, MY SANCTUARY

My church isn't just where I worship — it's where I was restored.

It's a sanctuary for the wounded soul and a launching pad for spiritual destiny.

Here, I have encountered God in ways that healed my past, empowered my present, and shaped the ministry I've been called to steward.

sssssschallenged me in my growth.

It taught me that deliverance isn't just an event — it's a lifestyle.

The teachings, the intercession, and the community support equipped me not only to receive healing but to minister healing to others.

My church gave me language for my pain and boldness for my calling.

I found family where I once found rejection.

I found purpose where I once carried shame.

Every prayer meeting, every altar call, every whispered "Yes, Lord" became a brick in the foundation of my new life.

When I look around the sanctuary, I see evidence of God's mercy in every seat.

People who were once bound now dance in freedom.

Those who once wept in silence now worship without fear.

This is holy ground — not because of the walls, but because of the transformation that happens within them.

I have learned that church is not about perfection; it's about presence — the presence of God that meets us where we are and makes us whole.

Here I found my voice again.

Here I found belonging.

Here I found restoration that lasts.

CHAPTER 8

BREAKING ADDICTION: A JOURNEY TO FREEDOM

Addiction does not start in the hands — it starts in the heart.

It begins when pain looks for comfort and finds a counterfeit.

For years I carried secret battles that no one saw, while smiling through service and ministry.

What I called relief was really retreat.

But the Holy Spirit was patient; He pursued me even in the places I tried to hide.

Deliverance came when I admitted I couldn't fix myself.

Freedom began when I stopped asking *why* and started saying *help*.

God met me in the stillness between failure and faith, and He began to peel away the layers of dependence one by one.

It wasn't instant — it was daily surrender.

I learned that addiction is not just about substances; it's about substitution.

Every bottle, every habit, every distraction was a way of filling a spiritual hunger.

Only the presence of God could satisfy that craving.

The day I let Him touch the wound beneath the habit, the chain broke.

No deliverance line, no spotlight — just a whispered *"Enough"* from Heaven and the courage to obey.

Since that day, I've walked free — not because I'm strong, but because His grace holds me steady.

Now I minister to those still caught between shame and surrender.

I tell them, *"God can handle your truth."*

Healing begins when honesty enters the room.

Freedom lasts when you guard your atmosphere, feed your faith, and stay accountable to the Spirit who saved you.

This chapter is not about my addiction; it's about His deliverance.

The same Spirit who raised Jesus from the dead raised me from the pit of dependence — and He can raise you too.

CHAPTER 9

RESTORATION OF FAITH AND SPIRITUAL AUTHORITY

There was a time when I believed my calling was over.

I had fallen, failed, and faded into the background of ministry life — still showing up, but not shining.

I thought I had disappointed God beyond repair.

But He reminded me that restoration isn't about reputation; it's about relationship.

Faith began to rise again, not through applause, but through obedience.

The same God who saved me in the beginning was saving me again — not from addiction or shame this time, but from disbelief.

He was rebuilding my faith, brick by brick, prayer by prayer.

God began speaking again.

His voice wasn't loud — it was gentle, clear, and sure.

He said, *"You are still called."*

That sentence alone broke the weight of years.

I started ministering again — not from ambition, but from assignment.

My spiritual authority didn't come from a title; it came from testimony.

The oil of my anointing flowed from endurance, not ease.

And in that authority, I began to see lives change.

Every altar I served at became sacred.

Every soul I prayed for reminded me that faith restored is faith refined.

God didn't give me a platform — He gave me purpose.

And with that purpose came a new kind of power: one grounded in humility, rooted in grace, and tested by fire.

Now when I preach, I preach from healed places.

When I lead, I lead from understanding.

When I serve, I serve knowing that everything I lost was preparation for what I now carry.

This chapter is for the one who thinks it's too late — for the one who believes their calling expired.

Your authority is not gone; it's maturing.

Your faith is not broken; it's being rebuilt.

You are not disqualified — you are being refined.

CHAPTER 10

PROPHETIC RECOVERY: HEARING GOD AGAIN

When trauma echoes louder than truth, it can feel impossible to hear God clearly. But He never stopped speaking. His voice isn't lost— it's layered beneath the noise, waiting to be uncovered.

Prophetic recovery is not just about hearing again—it's about trusting again. Trusting that God still speaks to you. That your discernment is valid. That your spiritual ears weren't broken by the betrayal, just bruised by the silence.

I remember the moment I realized God was still whispering. It wasn't in a pulpit or a prayer line—it was in the quiet, when I was folding laundry and crying over a memory I couldn't shake. His words came like balm: *"I never stopped calling you." *

This chapter is for the ones who feel spiritually deaf. For the ones who second-guess every impression, every dream, every nudge. For the ones who were told they were "too emotional" or "too deep" when they were actually prophetic.

Recovery begins with permission. Permission to hear God again. Permission to believe that your spiritual gifts weren't revoked—they were refined. Permission to prophesy healing over yourself before you ever speak it over others.

Let's clear the noise.

Let's reclaim the whisper.

Let's recover the voice of God in your life.

He's still speaking.

You're still chosen.

And your ears still work.

CHAPTER 11

THE ANATOMY OF HEALING: SPIRIT, SOUL, AND STRATEGY

Healing is not random—it's layered, intentional, and divine. It touches every part of who we are: spirit, soul, and body. But too often, we try to heal one layer while ignoring the others.

Spiritual healing begins with surrender. Not just to God's will, but to His timing. It's the moment we stop performing and start receiving. It's the quiet yes that breaks generational chains.

Soul healing requires truth-telling. Naming the trauma. Confronting the patterns. Releasing the shame. It's the work of therapy, prayer, journaling, and sometimes tears that won't stop flowing.

Strategic healing is where legacy begins. It's the curriculum, the workbook, the podcast, the outreach. It's the structure that turns your testimony into a tool. It's the system that makes healing transferable.

This chapter is for the ones who've done the spiritual work but still feel stuck. For the ones who've journaled and prayed but haven't built the strategy. For the ones who are ready to move from healing to helping.

Let's name the layers.

Let's honor the process.

Let's build the system that makes healing last.

CHAPTER 12

LEGACY HEALING:
WHEN YOUR STORY BECOMES
SOMEONE ELSE'S SURVIVAL

There comes a moment when your healing is no longer just about you. It becomes a lifeline for someone else. A roadmap. A mirror. A ministry.

Legacy healing is when your scars become sacred. When your journals become curriculum. When your silence becomes a sermon. It's the shift from "I survived" to "You will too."

I didn't write these chapters to impress anyone. I wrote them because I remember what it felt like to be invisible. To be wounded in the name of holiness. To be gifted but muzzled. And I promised God that if He healed me, I'd help heal others.

This chapter is for the ones who are ready to release. Ready to publish. Ready to coach. Ready to teach. Ready to build the archive that outlives them.

Your story is not just powerful—it's prophetic.

Your healing is not just personal—it's generational.

Your voice is not just restored—it's assigned.

Let's build the legacy.

Let's release the archive.

Let's make healing transferable.

CHAPTER 13

THE MINISTRY OF BELONGING: RESTORING THE DISPLACED

Belonging is more than attendance—it's spiritual adoption. It's the feeling of being seen, known, and valued. And for many, it's the very thing the church forgot to offer.

I've ministered to the displaced: the youth who aged out of foster care, the widows who lost their covering, the families who were silenced by shame. They didn't need a sermon—they needed a seat. A place where their story wasn't a liability but a legacy.

The ministry of belonging begins with invitation. Not just to a service, but to a safe space. It's the flyer, the phone call, the prayer line, the podcast episode that says, *"You're not forgotten."*

This chapter is for the ones who've been spiritually homeless. For the ones who've wandered from pew to pew, hoping someone would ask their name. For the ones who've been gifted but never affirmed.

You belong here.

Your story matters.

And your healing has a home.

Let's restore the displaced.

Let's rebuild the welcome.

Let's make ministry feel like family.

CHAPTER 14

VOICE RESTORATION: WHEN SILENCE BREAKS AND POWER RETURNS

There's a sound that hell fears—and it's your voice. Not just your volume, but your authority. Your testimony. Your prophetic tone. Your healing cadence.

Voice restoration is not just about speaking again—it's about reclaiming what was stolen. The confidence. The clarity. The call. It's the moment you stop whispering your truth and start declaring it.

I've coached women who hadn't prayed aloud in years. Men who hadn't sung since the funeral. Youth who were told they were "too much" or "too loud." And I watched God restore every octave, every utterance, every anointed phrase.

This chapter is for the ones who've been silenced by shame, grief, or spiritual abuse. For the ones who used to lead worship, preach, or teach—but now sit quietly, wondering if their voice still matters.

It does.

It always did.

And it's time to release it.

Let's restore the voice.

Let's break the silence.

Let's release the sound of healing.

CHAPTER 15

CURRICULUM AS CALLING: STRUCTURING THE HEALING

Healing is holy—but structure makes it transferable. When God gives you revelation, He also gives you responsibility: to organize it, teach it, and release it.

Curriculum is not just content—it's calling. It's the workbook, the facilitator guide, the branded insert that turns your testimony into a tool. It's the system that helps others walk through what you survived.

I didn't build curriculum because I wanted to be impressive. I built it because I saw too many people stuck in cycles. I knew that healing needed steps, not just sermons. And I knew that my story could be sequenced into strategy.

This chapter is for the ones who feel the nudge to teach. For the ones who've journaled for years but never published. For the ones who've coached informally but never built the framework.

Your healing has a structure.

Your story has a syllabus.

And your calling has a curriculum.

Let's build it.

Let's brand it.

Let's release it.

CHAPTER 16

HEALING FOR THE HEALERS: WHEN THE STRONG NEED RESTORATION

The ones who carry others often forget to care for themselves. The intercessors. The pastors. The coaches. The mothers. The mentors. The ones who pour out until they're empty.

Healing for the healers is not weakness—it's wisdom. It's the moment you admit that even strong vessels need refilling. That even anointed voices need rest. That even legacy leaders need space to grieve. I've ministered while mourning. Taught while tired. Coached while broken. And God met me in every moment—not with rebuke, but with restoration.

This chapter is for the ones who lead with excellence but cry in secret. For the ones who are celebrated privately but feel unseen publicly. For the ones who've been strong for everyone else and now need strength for themselves.

You're allowed to rest.

You're allowed to heal.

You're allowed to receive.

Let's restore the healers.

Let's refill the vessels.

Let's honor the ones who carry others.

CHAPTER 17

THE ARCHIVE OF IMPACT: PRESERVING WHAT GOD BUILT THROUGH YOU

Legacy is not just what you leave—it's what you organize, protect, and release. The archive is where healing becomes history. Where testimony becomes template. Where ministry becomes movement.

I built my archive because I knew the next generation would need it. Not just my children, but the displaced youth, the recovering families, the wounded leaders. I wanted them to have more than memories—I wanted them to have materials.

This chapter is for the ones who are ready to preserve. Ready to file the manuscripts. Ready to label the folders. Ready to build the digital vault that holds every flyer, workbook, podcast, and prayer.

Your archive is sacred.

Your impact is measurable.

And your legacy is ready.

Let's preserve the work.

Let's protect the voice.

Let's prepare the next generation.

CHAPTER 18

THE SOUND OF REVIVAL: WHEN HEALING BECOMES ATMOSPHERE

Revival doesn't begin with a crowd—it begins with a cry. It's the sound of one soul saying, "I'm ready." The sound of healing echoing through a sanctuary, a podcast, a prayer line. It's not just music—it's movement.

I've watched revival break out in living rooms, on phone calls, in coaching sessions. Not because of a pulpit, but because of presence. When God shows up, healing becomes atmosphere. And when healing becomes atmosphere, revival is inevitable.

This chapter is for the ones who carry sound. Worship leaders. Intercessors. Podcasters. Coaches. For the ones who know that revival isn't hype—it's holy.

Let's release the sound.

Let's host the healing.

Let's steward the revival.

CHAPTER 19

FINAL BENEDICTION: A PRAYER FOR THE HEALED

Lord, thank You for every reader who made it to this page.

Thank You for the tears they shed, the truths they faced, and the healing they received.

Thank You for the little girl in the corner, the wounded soul, the silenced voice—now restored.

I declare that this book will not just be read—it will be remembered.

That every testimony will become a tool.

That every scar will become sacred.

That every reader will rise.

Let this benediction be a release.

Let it be a sending.

Let it be a seal.

You are healed.

You are whole.

You are ready.

Amen.

CHAPTER 20

WORKBOOK:

The Wounded Soul Workbook:

This workbook is your space to process, write, and walk out what God began through *The Wounded Soul*.

Each page is an invitation to engage with the lessons, scriptures, and revelations you've read—turning understanding into transformation.

Here, **you become the co-author of your healing.**

Your story matters. Your reflections have power.

This is where revelation becomes reflection—and reflection becomes restoration.

HOW TO USE THIS WORKBOOK

- **Take your time.** There's no deadline for healing.

- **Write honestly.** No one will read these pages but you and God.

- **Pray before each exercise.** Ask the Holy Spirit to reveal what's hidden and heal what's hurting.

- **Revisit often.** Healing is layered—what you discover today may deepen tomorrow.

SECTION 1 — *Naming Your Wounds*

Before God can heal what's broken, we must name it.

Write freely—don't edit or explain. Honesty is the first step toward wholeness.

Reflection Questions:

1. What wound still shapes how I see myself or others?

2. When did I first learn to hide my pain instead of expressing it?

3. What message did my silence teach me about worth?

Scripture Meditation:

"He heals the brokenhearted and binds up their wounds." — *Psalm 147:3*

Journal Space:

(Use these lines to write your reflections.)

SECTION 2 — *Releasing Shame*

Shame binds the soul; grace breaks the chain.

This section helps you release guilt and step into acceptance.

Reflection Questions:

1. What moments do I still replay in regret?

2. What truth does God speak over that memory?

3. What would it look like to forgive myself?

Practical Step:

Write a forgiveness letter—to yourself, to someone else, or to your past. You don't need to send it. Just release it.

Scripture Meditation:

"Therefore, there is now no condemnation for those who are in Christ Jesus." — Romans 8:1

Journal Space:

(Use these lines to write your letter.)

SECTION 3 — *Rebuilding Identity*

You are not what happened to you—you are who God says you are.

This section helps you rebuild a healthy identity grounded in truth.

Reflection Questions:

1. What labels have I believed that God never gave me?

2. What does "new creation" mean to me personally?

3. What gifts or qualities reflect the real me beneath the pain?

Affirmation:

"I am chosen, cherished, and created with purpose."

Action Step:

List three affirmations you'll speak over yourself each morning this week.

SECTION 4 — *Restoring Voice*

Every healed heart deserves to speak.

This section focuses on rediscovering your spiritual and emotional voice.

Reflection Questions:

1. Where have I silenced myself out of fear or rejection?

2. How can I use my story to encourage others?

3. What truth do I need to speak—out loud—today?

Scripture Meditation:

"Let the redeemed of the Lord tell their story." — Psalm 107:2

Practical Step:

Record yourself reading one of your journal entries or favorite scriptures aloud. Listen to the power in your voice.

_____

_____

_____

_____

SECTION 5 — *Activating Legacy*

Healing doesn't end with you—it flows through you.

Legacy is what happens when your testimony becomes someone else's survival guide.

Reflection Questions:

1. Who can I share my story or journey with this month?

2. What part of my healing could help my family, community, or church?

3. What would I want my legacy of faith and restoration to be?

Action Step:

Design a "Legacy List." Write five things you'll build, teach, or pass on as part of your healing story.

FINAL REFLECTION

You've walked through pain, truth, surrender, and faith.

Now write your own declaration of healing—a closing statement of who you are today.

My Declaration:

"I am whole. I am healed. I am walking in purpose.

What once broke me now builds me.

What once silenced me now speaks through me.

My wounded soul has become a well of restoration."

Journal Space:

(Use these lines to write your declaration.)

_____

_____

_____

_____

_____

_____

_____

_____

_____

CLOSING PRAYER

Lord, thank You for every revelation, every tear, and every breakthrough written in these pages.

Seal the work You've begun. Let these words become living testimony.

Use this healed heart to heal others.

Amen.